Busy Ant Maths

Pupil Book 4A

Series Editor: Peter Clarke

Authors: Elizabeth Jurgensen, Jeanette Mumford, Sandra Roberts

Contents

4-digit numbers (1)

Recognise the place value of each digit in a 4-digit number

Challenge 1

1 Write the 3-digit numbers shown by the Base 10.

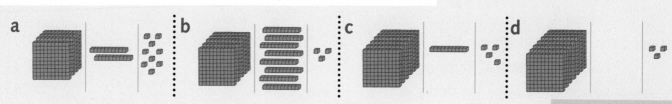

a   b   c   d

2 Write the place value of each digit in these numbers.

> **Example**
>
> 753 = 700 + 50 + 3

a 538   b 413   c 681   d 390   e 759   f 827

Challenge 2

1 Write the place value of each digit in these numbers.

> **Example**
>
> 4736 = 4000 + 700 + 30 + 6

a 1295   b 2861   c 2649   d 3804   e 3382   f 4741

2 These numbers have been separated into 1000s, 100s, 10s and 1s. What is each number?

a   4000   600   70   5   b   3000   200   30   7

c   5000   500   40   2   d   2000   700   10   8

Challenge 3

1 What numbers have been separated into 1000s, 100s, 10s and 1s?

I'm thinking of a number ...

a   20   400   1   5000   b   9   3000   10   600   c   4000   30   200   6

2 I'm thinking of a number. The 1000s digit is lower than 4. The 100s digit is 4. The 10s digit is even. The 1s digit is 6. Find eight possible numbers.

4-digit numbers (2)

Recognise the place value of each digit in a 4-digit number

Challenge 1

Write the 4-digit numbers shown by the Base 10.

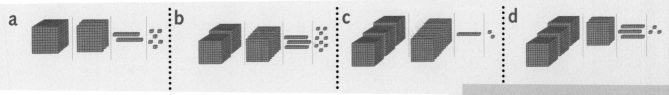

a   b   c   d

Challenge 2

1   Write the place value of each digit in these numbers.

Example
$1352 = 1000 + 300 + 50 + 2$

a   1247   b   2319   c   3184   d   3072   e   4713

2   Write the numbers represented by the money.

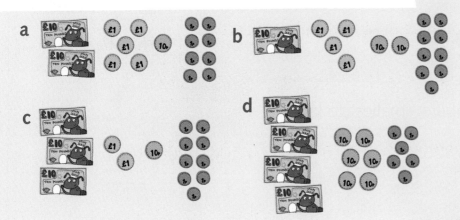

a   b   e

c   d

Challenge 3

1   I am thinking of a number. What is it?

a It has one 1, eight 10s, nine 100s and five 1000s.

b It has four 100s, nine 1000s, six 1s and five 10s.

c It has eight 1000s, three 1s, seven 100s and two 10s.

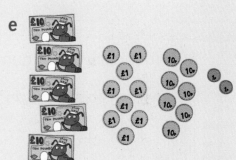

I'm thinking of a number ...

2   What would be a good way to estimate the number of leaves on a tree?

Ordering numbers beyond 1000

Order and compare numbers beyond 1000

Challenge 1

1 Order each set of numbers, smallest to largest.

   a 476, 286, 361, 582, 234   b 511, 151, 501, 155, 265

   c 755, 573, 675, 505, 615   d 287, 631, 167, 278, 218

   e 3621, 1467, 4255, 2854   f 2765, 1432, 3362, 4106

2 These numbers are in order. What could the missing numbers be?

   a 287, 295, ▲, 325, □, 361   b ▲, 388, ○, 415, △, 444

   c 623, ●, ■, 698, △, △   d 1000, ○, 1087, ■, 1104, ▲

   e 1254, ■, 1290, ▲, 1299, ○   f 2500, ○, 2530, ▲, ○, 2580

Challenge 2

1 Order each set of numbers, smallest to largest.

   a 4861, 2762, 1572, 3265   b 5087, 4206, 5208, 4062

   c 4261, 4482, 4166, 4528   d 5207, 5057, 5177, 5507

   e 4012, 5015, 5011, 4015   f 6643, 6628, 6649, 6612

2 a Use the number cards to make ten different 4-digit numbers.

   b Put the numbers in order, smallest to largest.

Challenge 3

Use the four number cards to make as many different 4-digit
numbers as you can.

Organise your numbers in a systematic way to help.
How many numbers can you make?

1000s more or less

Find 1000 more or less than a given number

Challenge 1

1 Write the number that is 1000 more than these numbers.

   a 365   b 276   c 831   d 3671   e 2995   f 4329

2 Write the number that is 1000 less than these numbers.

   a 3825   b 3199   c 4794   d 4067   e 4326   f 5439

Challenge 2

1 Write the number that is 2000 more than these numbers.

   a 3284   b 2862   c 3192   d 4629   e 5928   f 2690

2 Write the number that is 2000 less than these numbers.

   a 5722   b 5063   c 4762   d 3981   e 6109   f 7321

3 a Write six 4-digit numbers greater than 2000.

   b On either side of your number, write the number
      that is 2000 less and 2000 more.

Example		
2877	4877	6877

Challenge 3

1 Write the numbers that are 3000 more and less than these numbers.

   a 6341   b 3842   c 5999   d 4025   e 5827   f 6297

2 a Write six 4-digit numbers greater than 4000.

   b On either side of your number, write the number
      that is 4000 less and 4000 more.

Example		
877	4877	8877

7

Mental addition

Use mental methods for addition

Challenge 1

a 243 + 40	b 226 + 70	c 357 + 30	d 425 + 60
e 372 + 40	f 351 + 80	g 462 + 70	h 438 + 80
i 263 + 300	j 421 + 400	k 514 + 200	l 167 + 500
m 285 + 600	n 493 + 400	o 332 + 200	p 428 + 500

Challenge 2

Work out these calculations. Which can you do mentally?

a 479 + 80	b 424 + 500	c 682 + 70	d 516 + 80
e 372 + 600	f 173 + 700	g 945 + 90	h 286 + 800
i 140 + 38	j 190 + 62	k 270 + 58	l 320 + 67
m 470 + 173	n 510 + 197	o 560 + 172	p 590 + 165

Challenge 3

1 Work out these calculations. Which can you do mentally?

a 670 + 183	b 740 + 196	c 770 + 182	d 830 + 166
e 680 + 272	f 540 + 289	g 690 + 271	h 740 + 285
i 810 + 229	j 870 + 281	k 950 + 257	l 1050 + 237
m 1030 + 252	n 1080 + 328	o 1250 + 426	p 1370 + 538

2 Explain how to add mentally a 3-digit number and a 3- or 4-digit multiple of 10.

Mental subtraction

Use mental methods for subtraction

Challenge 1

a 176 – 40   b 253 – 30   c 247 – 40   d 283 – 60

e 235 – 60   f 213 – 40   g 346 – 50   h 362 – 80

i 365 – 200   j 428 – 200   k 481 – 300   l 537 – 300

m 529 – 400   n 631 – 200   o 617 – 400   p 682 – 300

Challenge 2

Work out these calculations. Which can you do mentally?

a 462 – 200   b 451 – 70   c 588 – 90   d 407 – 70

e 583 – 300   f 627 – 60   g 761 – 80   h 743 – 500

i 372 – 130   j 385 – 180   k 467 – 150   l 428 – 140

m 483 – 210   n 538 – 230   o 581 – 250   p 549 – 280

Challenge 3

1 Work out these calculations. Which can you do mentally?

a 537 – 250   b 586 – 310   c 693 – 270   d 715 – 240

e 783 – 260   f 801 – 180   g 846 – 270   h 956 – 360

i 984 – 330   j 927 – 310   k 968 – 370   l 1007 – 220

m 1067 – 250   n 1038 – 180   o 1154 – 130   p 1285 – 940

2 Explain how to subtract a 3-digit multiple of 10 from a 3- or 4-digit number.

1-step problems

Solve 1-step word problems in contexts

SCHOOL PLAY
Wednesday night

The children in Year 3 and Year 4 are taking part in a school play.

Challenge 1

1 On Wednesday, 68 tickets had been sold in advance but then 200 people arrived to buy tickets on the evening. How many people watched the play on Wednesday?

2 Year 4 always make the drinks to sell. They have prepared 150 cups of orange juice and 72 cups of apple juice. How many drinks have they made?

3 There were 224 seats put out for the play. 20 minutes before the play started, 70 were full. How many were still empty?

Challenge 2

1 140 seats had been put out in the hall, but 243 tickets had been sold. How many more seats did they need?

2 There were cookies for sale on Saturday evening. The stall started with 435 cookies and sold 240. How many were left?

3 On Friday evening 310 tickets were sold, on Saturday 168 tickets were sold. How many tickets were sold in total?

4 Thursday evening was when Year 3 and Year 4 parents came to see the play. 372 tickets had been sold. Year 3 parents had bought 190 of them. How many had Year 4 parents bought?

Challenge 3

1 Popcorn is always popular at the play. Year 3 made 665 bags to sell. After one night they had 365 bags left. How many had they sold?

2 Year 4 had prepared 486 cups of juice to sell one evening, but then the table collapsed and 190 were spilt. How many were left?

3 In total, 984 tickets were sold. On Thursday, 370 were sold. How many were sold on the other nights?

2-step problems

Solve 2-step word problems in contexts

The children in Year 3 and 4 are taking part in a school play.

Challenge 1

1 On Thursday Year 3 sold 45 tickets, on Friday they sold 80 tickets and on Saturday they sold 200 tickets. How many did they sell altogether?

2 The first part of the play lasted 63 minutes and the second part lasted 59 minutes. The interval was 30 minutes. How long did the whole play last, including the interval?

3 Year 4 made 300 cakes to sell. 48 were sold on Thursday and 170 on Friday. How many were left?

Challenge 2

1 On Thursday Year 4 sold 163 tickets, on Friday they sold 140 tickets and on Saturday they sold 300 tickets. How many did they sell altogether?

2 The popcorn was selling quickly. At 7 p.m. there were 300 packs. By 7.30 p.m. 137 had been sold. By 8.00 p.m. another 162 were sold. How many were left?

3 The school printed 430 programmes. On Thursday they sold 274, and 150 were sold the next night. How many were left?

4 After the play on Saturday the 340 seats had to be put away. 60 were put away in the morning, and 73 at lunchtime. How many were still out?

Challenge 3

1 In the week before the play the children spent 320 minutes rehearsing. They did 125 minutes on Monday, 94 minutes on Tuesday and the rest on Wednesday. How long was Wednesday's rehearsal?

2 The school hopes to raise £450 from the play. They made £238 on Thursday and £170 on Friday. How much more do they need to reach their target?

3 The teachers helped with the preparations for the play. They spent 98 minutes decorating the hall, 260 minutes getting the stage ready and 380 minutes making the costumes. How long did their preparations take?

Symmetry in 2-D shapes

Identify lines of symmetry in 2-D shapes

You will need:
• mirror

Lines of symmetry	Road sign
None	
1	
More than 1	

Challenge 1

Place your mirror on each road sign in turn to check for lines of symmetry. Copy and complete the table.

Example

Challenge 2

Use your mirror to test each shape.
Write the letters of the 2-D shapes that:

1 Have no lines of symmetry.

2 Have 1 line of symmetry.

3 Have more than 1 line of symmetry.

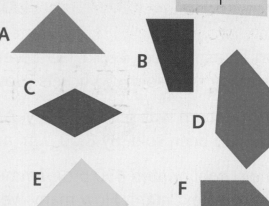

Challenge 3

How many different symmetrical shapes can you make using six interlocking squares each time?

1 Draw each shape you make on squared paper.

2 Mark the line or lines of symmetry on each shape with a dotted red line.

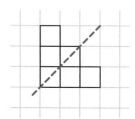

You will need:
• six interlocking squares in the same colour
• squared paper
• ruler
• red pencil

12

Reflecting 2-D shapes

Reflect 2-D shapes along a line of symmetry

lenge 1

Place your mirror along the line of symmetry. Write the name of the shape you make.

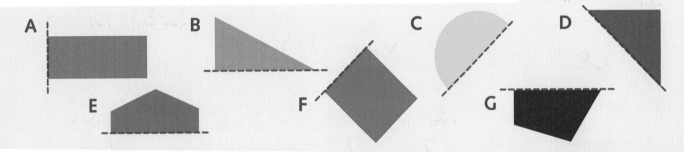

lenge 2

1 These shapes are halves of shapes. For each shape, draw two possible whole shapes on squared dot paper.

You will need:
• squared dot paper
• five interlocking square tiles
• ruler
• red pencil

2 Work with a partner.

a Take five interlocking square tiles each and make a T-shape.

b Find how many different symmetrical shapes you can make by joining both T-shapes together.

c Record each shape you make on squared dot paper.

d Mark the line or lines of symmetry with a dotted red line.

Example

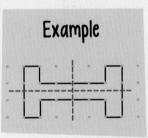

llenge 3

Imagine that the four shapes in Question 1 of Challenge 2 are all quarters of shapes.

1 For each shape, find as many different whole shapes as you can.

2 Record your shapes on squared dot paper and mark the lines of symmetry in red.

You will need:
• squared dot paper
• ruler
• red pencil

Completing symmetrical patterns

Complete simple symmetrical patterns using lines of symmetry

Challenge 1

1 Copy each pattern on to squared paper.

2 Colour the blank squares to make each pattern symmetrical.

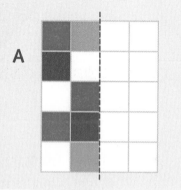
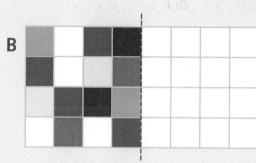
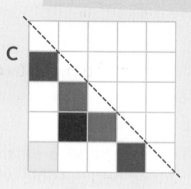

Challenge 2

1 For each grid below, copy the dots and line of symmetry on to squared paper.

2 Draw the reflected image of the dots:

a in 1 line of symmetry for grids **A–D**.

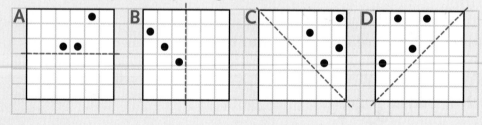

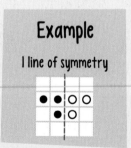

Example

1 line of symmetry

b in 2 lines of symmetry for grids **E–H**.

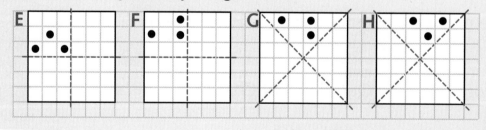

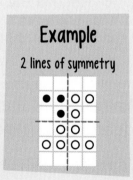

Example

2 lines of symmetry

Challenge 3

Design a logo for a smartphone games app. Your logo should have 2 lines of symmetry.

Making repeating patterns

Make patterns by reflecting shapes in vertical lines of symmetry

This pattern is made by reflecting a shape in vertical lines of symmetry.

- Copy each shape below on to squared paper.

- Mark the lines of symmetry of each shape with dotted red lines.

- Reflect the shape to continue the pattern.

You will need:
- squared paper
- ruler
- red pencil
- coloured pencils

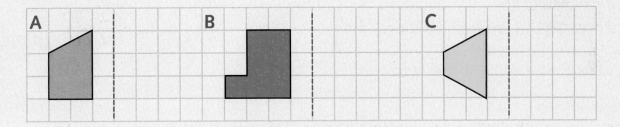

- Copy each shape below on to squared paper.

- Mark the lines of symmetry of each shape with dotted red lines.

- Reflect the shape to continue the pattern.

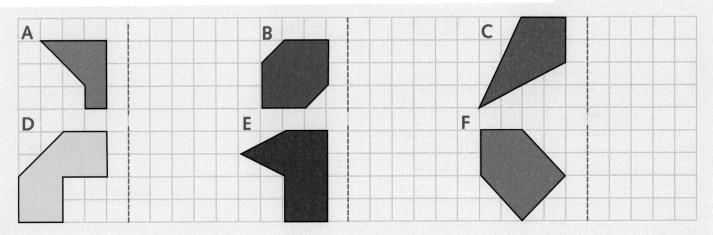

Investigate the repeating patterns you can make by reflecting the following:

a an 8-sided shape in vertical lines of symmetry

b the complete pattern of your 8-sided shape in a horizontal line of symmetry

15

9 multiplication table

Recall the multiplication and division facts for the 9 multiplication table

Some of the multiples of 9 have been written incorrectly in this number grid. Rewrite the number grid correctly in order, smallest to largest.

27	30	16	84
36	45	90	53
61	72	28	9

1 Write down which of the key facts you would use to answer the multiplication facts below. Then write the answers to these facts.

$1 \times 9 =$

$2 \times 9 =$

$10 \times 9 =$

$5 \times 9 =$

a $9 \times 9 =$ b $4 \times 9 =$ c $3 \times 9 =$

d $6 \times 9 =$ e $8 \times 9 =$ f $7 \times 9 =$

2 a ■ $\times 9 = 27$ b $6 \times$ ● $= 72$ c $9 \times$ ▢ $= 63$ d ■ $\times 9 = 36$

e $11 \times$ ▲ $= 99$ f $108 = 9 \times$ ●   g ▲ $\times 9 = 81$ h $18 \div$ ■ $= 9$

i $54 \div$ ● $= 9$ j ▲ $\div 9 = 5$ k $36 =$ ■ $\times 9$ l $27 \div$ ▲ $= 3$

m ▢ $\div 9 = 10$ n ● $\times 9 = 45$ o $63 \div$ ▲ $= 9$ p △ $\div 9 = 8$

Read the clues to find the numbers.

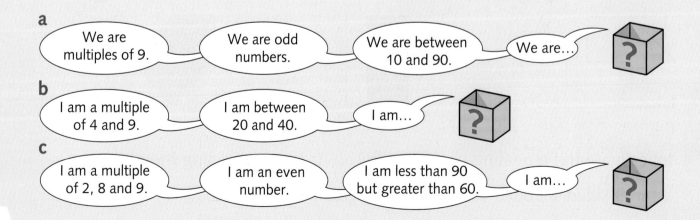

a
We are multiples of 9.   We are odd numbers.   We are between 10 and 90.   We are...   ?

b
I am a multiple of 4 and 9.   I am between 20 and 40.   I am...   ?

c
I am a multiple of 2, 8 and 9.   I am an even number.   I am less than 90 but greater than 60.   I am...   ?

Using the 10 multiplication table to learn the 9 multiplication table

Recall the multiplication and division facts for the 9 multiplication table

Challenge 1

1 Write the previous multiple of 9.

    a 18   b 45   c 36   d 81   e 90

2 Write the next multiple of 9.

    a 45   b 18   c 72   d 36   e 27

Challenge 2

1 Write the multiples of 9 that are two multiples of 9 more and less than these numbers.

    a 63   b 27   c 72   d 108   e 81   f 54

2 Write a multiplication fact for each number coming out of the machine.

Challenge 3

For each dartboard, multiply the number in the pink section by 9. Then multiply your answer by the number in the blue section.

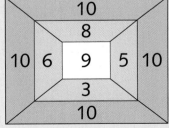

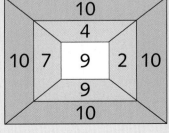

6 multiplication table

Recall the multiplication and division facts for
the 6 multiplication table

Write down which of the key facts you would use to answer
the multiplication facts below. Then write the answers to these facts.

a $9 \times 6 =$ b $7 \times 6 =$ c $4 \times 6 =$

d $6 \times 6 =$ e $3 \times 6 =$ f $8 \times 6 =$

1 One number in each trio is missing. Work out the missing number in each set
of trios, then write two multiplication and two division facts for each.

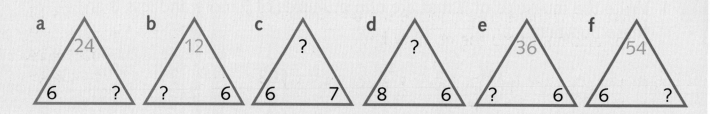

a 24 / 6 ?   b 12 / ? 6   c ? / 6 7   d ? / 8 6   e 36 / ? 6   f 54 / 6 ?

2 a $\blacksquare \times 6 = 30$ b $6 \times \triangle = 24$ c $6 \times \blacksquare = 36$ d $\bullet \times 6 = 42$

e $12 \times \triangle = 72$ f $6 = 6 \times \bigcirc$ g $48 \div \blacktriangle = 6$ h $\square \div 6 = 3$

i $54 = \bigcirc \times 6$ j $12 \div \blacksquare = 2$ k $\blacksquare \div 6 = 11$ l $42 \div \bullet = 6$

Read the clues to find the numbers.

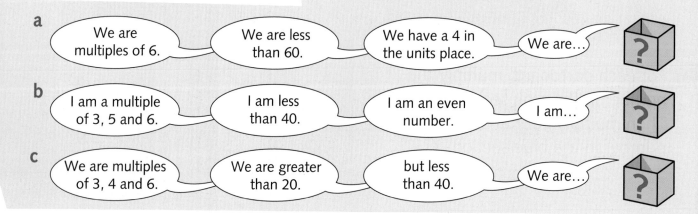

a We are multiples of 6.   We are less than 60.   We have a 4 in the units place.   We are…

b I am a multiple of 3, 5 and 6.   I am less than 40.   I am an even number.   I am…

c We are multiples of 3, 4 and 6.   We are greater than 20.   but less than 40.   We are…

Using other multiplication tables to learn the 6 multiplication table

Recall multiplication and division facts for the 6 multiplication table

1 Copy and complete the number line for the 3 multiplication facts.

1	2	3	4	5	6	7	8	9	10	11	12

☐ ☐ ☐ 12 ☐ ☐ ☐ ☐ 27 ☐ ☐ ☐

Hint

Use your completed number lines to recite the 3 and 6 multiplication and division facts, e.g.
4 × 3 = 12,
27 ÷ 3 = 9,
4 × 6 = 24,
54 ÷ 6 = 9.

2 Double the answers to the 3 multiplication facts to work out the answers to the 6 multiplication facts. Copy and complete the number line.

1	2	3	4	5	6	7	8	9	10	11	12

☐ ☐ ☐ 24 ☐ ☐ ☐ ☐ 54 ☐ ☐ ☐

Example

6 x 6

(6 x 4) (6 x 2)

24 + 12 = 36

or

6 x 6

(6 x 5) (6 x 1)

30 + 6 = 36

Use the strategy shown to write the answer to the 6 multiplication calculations.

a   4 x 6   b   9 x 6   c   3 x 6   d   7 x 6

e   8 x 6   f   7 x 6   g   12 x 6   h   9 x 6

Write a multiplication fact for each number coming out of the machine.

a
40
90
30
80
70

x6

b
240
360
540
600
420

÷6

Equivalent fractions (1)

Recognise and show, using diagrams, families of common equivalent fractions

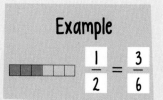

Example

$$\frac{1}{2} = \frac{3}{6}$$

Challenge 1

Draw these diagrams and write the fraction equivalent to a half. Underneath write $\frac{1}{2} = \frac{}{}$

a   b

c   d

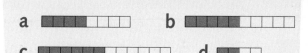

Challenge 2

1 Write the fractions equivalent to a half.

a   = $\frac{}{} = \frac{}{}$

Example

=

$$\frac{1}{2} = \frac{3}{6}$$

b   = $\frac{}{} = \frac{}{}$

c   = $\frac{}{} = \frac{}{}$

d   = $\frac{}{} = \frac{}{}$

e   = $\frac{}{} = \frac{}{}$

f   = $\frac{}{} = \frac{}{}$

2 Continue this pattern: $\dfrac{1}{2} = \dfrac{2}{4} = \dfrac{}{6} =$

Challenge 3

1 Write in the fractions equivalent to a quarter.

a   b   c

2 Continue the pattern without the diagrams. Stop at 48ths.

3 What do you notice about all of the equivalent fractions?

Equivalent fractions (2)

Recognise and show, using diagrams,
families of common equivalent fractions

Example

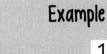 $\frac{1}{4} = \frac{2}{8}$

Challenge 1

Draw these diagrams and write the fraction
equivalent to a quarter. Underneath write $\frac{1}{4} = \frac{\ }{\ }$

a [diagram]   b [diagram]

c [diagram]   d [diagram]

Challenge 2

1 Write the fractions equivalent to a quarter.

a [diagram] = [diagram] $\frac{\ }{\ } = \frac{\ }{\ }$

b [diagram] = [diagram] $\frac{\ }{\ } = \frac{\ }{\ }$

c [diagram] = [diagram] $\frac{\ }{\ } = \frac{\ }{\ }$

d [diagram] = [diagram] $\frac{\ }{\ } = \frac{\ }{\ }$

e [diagram] = [diagram] $\frac{\ }{\ } = \frac{\ }{\ }$

2 Continue this pattern: $\frac{1}{4} = \frac{2}{8} = \frac{\ }{12} =$

Challenge 3

1 Write the fractions equivalent to three-quarters.

a [diagram]   b [diagram]   c [diagram]

2 Continue this pattern: $\frac{3}{4} = \frac{6}{8} = \frac{\ }{12} =$

3 Explain the pattern.

Non-unit fractions (1)

Understand the relation between non-unit fractions and multiplication and division

Challenge 1

Work out these unit fractions.

a $\frac{1}{2}$ of 22

b $\frac{1}{2}$ of 36

c $\frac{1}{2}$ of 80

d $\frac{1}{4}$ of 28

e $\frac{1}{4}$ of 48

f $\frac{1}{4}$ of 100

g $\frac{1}{3}$ of 24

h $\frac{1}{3}$ of 36

i $\frac{1}{3}$ of 42

j $\frac{1}{5}$ of 25

k $\frac{1}{5}$ of 35

l $\frac{1}{5}$ of 50

Challenge 2

1 Work out these non-unit fractions.

a $\frac{3}{4}$ of 12

b $\frac{3}{4}$ of 20

c $\frac{3}{4}$ of 32

d $\frac{3}{4}$ of 40

e $\frac{2}{3}$ of 18

f $\frac{2}{3}$ of 27

g $\frac{2}{3}$ of 39

h $\frac{2}{3}$ of 60

i $\frac{3}{5}$ of 30

j $\frac{3}{5}$ of 45

k $\frac{3}{5}$ of 60

l $\frac{3}{5}$ of 75

2 What is a non-unit fraction?

Challenge 3

1 Work out these non-unit fractions.

a $\frac{3}{4}$ of 60

b $\frac{2}{5}$ of 70

c $\frac{2}{3}$ of 90

d $\frac{3}{5}$ of 45

e $\frac{2}{6}$ of 54

f $\frac{4}{5}$ of 65

g $\frac{2}{5}$ of 70

h $\frac{4}{6}$ of 72

i $\frac{3}{5}$ of 65

j $\frac{5}{6}$ of 66

k $\frac{3}{6}$ of 48

l $\frac{4}{6}$ of 90

2 Explain how to find non-unit fractions of amounts.

Non-unit fractions (2)

Understand the relation between non-unit fractions and multiplication and division

Example

$\frac{3}{4}$ of 20

$20 \div 4 = 5$ ($\frac{1}{4}$ of 20)

$3 \times 5 = 15$

$\frac{3}{4}$ of 20 = 15

Challenge 1

Work out these non-unit fractions.

a $\frac{3}{4}$ of 12

b $\frac{3}{4}$ of 24

c $\frac{3}{4}$ of 40

d $\frac{2}{3}$ of 15

e $\frac{2}{3}$ of 21

f $\frac{2}{3}$ of 30

g $\frac{3}{5}$ of 20

h $\frac{3}{5}$ of 35

i $\frac{3}{5}$ of 40

j $\frac{2}{6}$ of 18

k $\frac{2}{6}$ of 30

l $\frac{2}{6}$ of 42

Challenge 2

1 Work out these non-unit fractions.

a $\frac{2}{6}$ of 78

b $\frac{2}{6}$ of 90

c $\frac{5}{6}$ of 102

d $\frac{4}{9}$ of 54

e $\frac{5}{9}$ of 81

f $\frac{7}{9}$ of 36

g $\frac{5}{8}$ of 96

h $\frac{3}{8}$ of 112

i $\frac{7}{8}$ of 128

j $\frac{4}{9}$ of 108

k $\frac{3}{4}$ of 92

l $\frac{4}{5}$ of 125

2 I have some counters. I halve them, then halve them again, then halve them again. Now there are 7 in each group. How many counters did I start with?

Challenge 3

1 Work out these non-unit fractions.

a $\frac{4}{6}$ of 138

b $\frac{5}{7}$ of 133

c $\frac{2}{8}$ of 128

d $\frac{4}{9}$ of 135

e $\frac{3}{7}$ of 147

f $\frac{6}{8}$ of 152

g $\frac{5}{6}$ of 150

h $\frac{7}{9}$ of 162

i $\frac{2}{7}$ of 168

j $\frac{8}{8}$ of 176

k $\frac{2}{3}$ of 198

l $\frac{3}{4}$ of 184

2 I have some money. I spend half at the bookshop, a quarter at the supermarket and an eighth on sweets. I have £3.25 left. How much money did I have to start with?

Translating a 2-D shape

Recognise where a shape will be after a translation

You will need:
- squared dot paper
- ruler

Challenges 1,2

Copy each shape **A–D** below on to squared dot paper. Translate each shape twice as follows:

  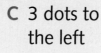 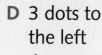

| **A** 3 dots to the right → | **B** 3 dots to the right → | **C** 3 dots to the left ← | **D** 3 dots to the left ← |

Example

3 dots to the right →

Challenges 2,3

1 Translate each shape above twice as follows:

a shapes **A** and **B** – 3 dots up

b shapes **C** and **D** – 3 dots down

2 Write the instructions to translate the blue quadrilateral to the new positions **A–F**.
The first one has been done for you.

Example

A: 3 dots to the left then 1 dot up.

Challenge 3

Make patterns by translating the coloured shape:

- to the right and to the left

- up and down, then to the right and to the left.

a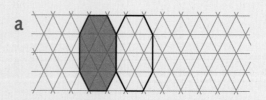

b

You will need:
- triangular grid paper
- coloured pencils
- ruler

24

Coordinates map

Use coordinates to describe the position of a point on a grid in the first quadrant

Example

Agent D is at the point (4, 3).

2,3 The map shows where six secret agents are looking for a buried transmitter.

Write the coordinates for:

Agent A (,)   Agent G (,)

Agent J (,)   Agent M (,)

Agent Z (,)

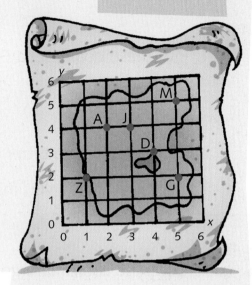

2

1 Agent B is at a position between Agents G and M. Write two coordinates that show where he might be.

2 Agent B has this secret code on his laptop. Read the coordinates to find out where the transmitter is buried. Each line is a new word.

(5,4) (5,1) (4,3)

(1,4) (1,1) (3,1) (5,1) (4,4)

(1,2) (3,4) (5,3) (3,3)

(2,1) (2,3) (1,1) (3,1) (1,3)

(3,4) (5,3) (3,1) (1,3)

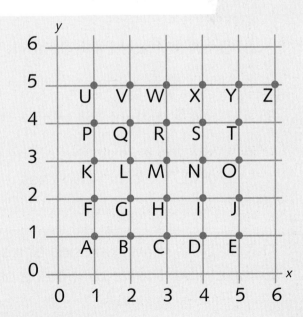

3 Using Agent B's secret code:

- Write your first name.

- Write in code where you would bury the transmitter, then ask a friend to read it.

Plotting the points

Plot specified points on a coordinate grid in the first quadrant

You will need:
- Resource 14: 6 × 6 coordinate grids
- ruler

1 Plot these points on a 6 × 6 coordinate grid.

    a (1,2), (6,6), (1,5)   **b** (2,2), (2,5), (6,5), (6,2)

2 Join the points in order with straight lines to make a 2-D shape.

3 Name the shape you make.

Example

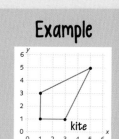

kite

1 Copy the coordinate grid. The points show 3 vertices of a square. Plot and write the 4th vertex of the square.

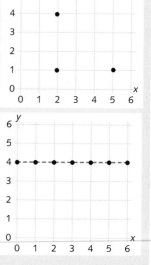

2 Copy the coordinate grid and the marked points.

    a Plot these points on the same grid: (3, 0), (3, 1), (3, 2), (3, 3), (3, 4) (3, 5).

    b Draw a straight line through the points.

    c Write the coordinates of the point that the lines intersect.

    d Draw a straight line joining the points (0, 0) and (6, 6).

    e Write the coordinates of the points where the diagonal line crosses the other two lines.

This diagram shows one side of a square.
Complete the square by plotting on the coordinate grid:

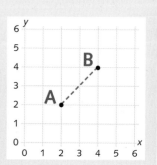

    a your first choice of vertices for points **C** and **D**

    b a 2nd set of vertices for points **C** and **D**.

Translations on a grid

Translate a shape on a coordinate grid in the first quadrant

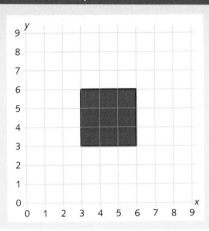

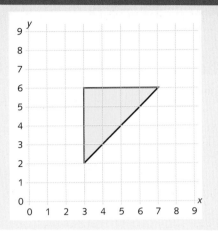

You will need:

- Resource 15: 9 × 9 coordinate grids
- ruler
- coloured pencil
- ICT tools (optional)

Challenges 1, 2

1 For each shape:

    a copy it on to a 9 × 9 coordinate grid

    b translate the shape 1 square right, 1 square down.

2 Colour the shape in the overlap and name the shape.

Example

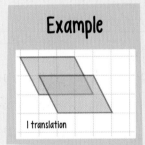

I translation

Challenge 2

Look at your answers to the Challenge 1, 2 activity. For each shape:

- Write the coordinates of the shape in the overlap.
- Translate the shape 1 square left and 1 square up.

Example

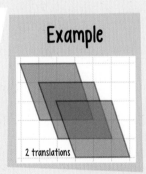

2 translations

Challenge 3

Copy the arrow on to a computer screen using ICT tools or on to a 9 × 9 coordinate grid. Translate the arrow as follows:

    a horizontally by adding 4 units to the x coordinate

    b vertically by adding 4 units to the y coordinate

    c diagonally by adding 4 units to the x and y coordinates.

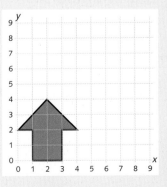

Addition chains

Use mental methods for addition

Put a start number at the beginning of the number chain.
Work out all the calculations.

Challenge 1

Start numbers:

a 370   b 450   c 520   d 560   e 640

Start number → ? → ? → ? → ? → ? → ? → ? → ?

+73   +4   +50   +8   +60   +200   +7   +124

Challenge 2

Start numbers:

a 370   b 450   c 520   d 560   e 640

Start number → ? → ? → ? → ? → ? → ? → ? → ?

+127   +200   +70   +9   +4   +142   +43   +6

Challenge 3

Start numbers:

a 370   b 450   c 520   d 560   e 640

Start number → ? → ? → ? → ? → ? → ? → ? → ?

+247   +7   +60   +43   +400   +9   +80   +58

Written addition (I)

- Add numbers with 3 digits using the formal written method of columnar addition
- Estimate the answer to a calculation

Work out the answer to each calculation using a written method for addition.

a	325 + 431	b	527 + 252
c	347 + 425	d	276 + 416
e	408 + 369	f	527 + 456
g	614 + 378	h	538 + 458
i	377 + 416	j	529 + 449

Estimate an answer for each calculation, then work out the answer.

a	562 + 384	b	471 + 476
c	548 + 435	d	375 + 564
e	459 + 434	f	637 + 428
g	753 + 639	h	862 + 684
i	791 + 757	j	836 + 548

Estimate an answer for each calculation, then work out the answer.

a	784 + 743	b	847 + 738	c	915 + 769
d	872 + 965	e	884 + 983	f	765 + 874
g	893 + 647	h	966 + 758	i	946 + 875
j	993 + 949	k	623 + 132 + 205	l	412 + 278 + 486

Written addition (2)

- Add numbers with up to 4 digits using the formal written method of columnar addition
- Estimate the answer to a calculation

Challenge 1

Work out the answer to each calculation using a written method for addition.

a 573 + 381
b 492 + 465
c 568 + 427
d 384 + 492
e 537 + 416
f 645 + 638
g 583 + 674
h 628 + 744
i 674 + 751
j 768 + 771

Challenge 2

Estimate an answer for each calculation, then work out the answer.

a 792 + 641
b 847 + 728
c 668 + 761
d 856 + 892
e 878 + 718
f 674 + 548
g 782 + 638
h 847 + 576
i 728 + 884
j 953 + 859

Challenge 3

Estimate an answer for each calculation, then work out the answer.

a 894 + 856
b 963 + 877
c 807 + 795
d 966 + 855
e 964 + 987
f 1372 + 1295
g 1248 + 1337
h 1368 + 1254
i 1638 + 1517
j 1572 + 1756

Leisure centre problems

Solve word problems in contexts, deciding which operations and methods to use and why

allenge 1

1 On Monday, 130 people swam in the morning and 142 used the pool in the afternoon. How many people swam altogether?

2 Year 4's target is to each swim 250 metres. Jack can swim 145 metres. How much further does he need to swim to meet the target?

3 The leisure centre took £437 on Friday and £215 on Saturday. How much money did they take altogether?

allenge 2

1 1 week Oliver swam 896 metres: 267 on Monday, 358 on Tuesday and the rest on Wednesday. How many metres did he swim on Wednesday?

2 The leisure centre shop has 620 pairs of goggles to sell. It sells 275 pairs on 1 day and 340 on the next day. How many pairs are left in the shop?

3 The shop has some swimming hats on special offer. It has 530 hats to sell. 236 are sold on 1 day so the manager orders another 420. How many will he have to sell?

4 439 people used the gym on 1 day, and 387 used the swimming pool. Out of these people, 256 did not pay as they had a free voucher. How many did pay?

allenge 3

1 The swimming pool has a leak. 3940 litres leaked out on Monday, 3677 leaked out on Tuesday and on Wednesday another 3570 litres leaked out. Fortunately, on Thursday the leak was fixed. How much water was lost?

2 The leisure centre is having a bad week. After the leaks were fixed the shop was burgled. The manager is working out how much money was taken. He knows that on Monday the shop made £1763 and on Tuesday it made £670. After the burglary he has £558 left. How much was stolen?

3 The manager of the leisure centre needs to know how much water is in the swimming pool, but he is not sure how to find out. What should he do?

Decimal fractions

- Understand the place value of tenths
- Recognise and write decimal equivalents for tenths

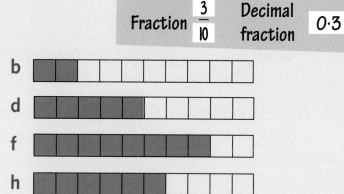
Example

Fraction $\dfrac{3}{10}$ Decimal fraction 0.3

Challenge 1

Count the tenths and record them as a fraction and a decimal fraction.

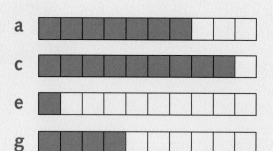

a

b

c

d

e

f

g

h

Challenge 2

1 Write the decimal fraction that is of equal value to these fractions.

a $\dfrac{3}{10}$ b $\dfrac{8}{10}$ c $\dfrac{1}{10}$ d $\dfrac{4}{10}$ e $\dfrac{7}{10}$

f $\dfrac{9}{10}$ g $\dfrac{5}{10}$ h $\dfrac{2}{10}$ i $\dfrac{6}{10}$ j $\dfrac{10}{10}$

2 Write the next tenth.

a 0·5   b 0·8   c 0·3   d 0·1   e 1·4

f 1·7   g 1·5   h 2·7   i 2·1   j 3·6

Challenge 3

1 What is the decimal fraction that is of equal value to these mixed numbers?

a $1\dfrac{3}{10}$ b $1\dfrac{7}{10}$ c $2\dfrac{4}{10}$ d $2\dfrac{8}{10}$ e $3\dfrac{1}{10}$

f $3\dfrac{9}{10}$ g $4\dfrac{5}{10}$ h $4\dfrac{6}{10}$ i $5\dfrac{4}{10}$ j $5\dfrac{2}{10}$

2 Draw the number line and write in the tenths as fractions and decimal fractions.

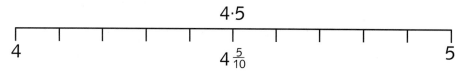

4·5

4    $4\dfrac{5}{10}$ 5

Comparing decimals

Compare decimals with 1 decimal place

1 Count on in tenths for five numbers from these decimals.

a 0·7	b 1·3	c 2·5
d 3·2	e 3·8	f 4
g 4·1	h 4·7	i 5·5

Example

0·2, 0·3, 0·4, 0·5, 0·6, 0·7

2

1 Put these decimal numbers in order, smallest to largest.

a 1·7, 1·3, 1·8, 1·1, 1·9   b 2·3, 2·8, 2·1, 2·5, 2·6   c 3·7, 3·2, 3·8, 3·1, 3·9

d 4·5, 4·7, 4·3, 4·6, 4·1   e 5·2, 5·6, 5·9, 5·3, 5·1   f 6·6, 6·1, 6·9, 6·7, 6·5

g 7·2, 7·7, 7·9, 7·3, 7·1   h 5·3, 2·7, 1·9, 4·6, 3·7   i 3·5, 2·6, 3·1, 2·5, 3·8

2 Write the decimal numbers that are one tenth smaller and one tenth larger than these numbers.

a 2·7	b 3·1	c 4·8	d 4·5	e 5·7
f 2·9	g 8·2	h 9·7	i 10	j 12·5

3

1 Fill in the spaces with decimal numbers, keeping the numbers in order.

a ___ , 7·7, ___ , 8·3, ___ , 9, ___ , 9·5   b 8·1 ___ , 8·5, ___ , 8·9, ___ , ___ , ___

c 9, ___ , ___ , 9·6, ___ , ___ , 10·2, ___   d 10, ___ , ___ , 10·7, ___ , ___ , 11·3

2 Write the less than < or greater than > sign between these pairs of numbers.

a 2·5 ___ 2·7	b 1·6 ___ 1·9	c 2·8 ___ 2·1	d 2 ___ 2·6
e 5·5 ___ 3·5	f 7·8 ___ 8·7	g 9·3 ___ 9·1	h 12·5 ___ 11·4

33

Rounding to the whole number

Round decimals with 1 decimal place to the nearest whole number

Challenge
1

1 Look at the decimal number on the number line.
What number should it round to?

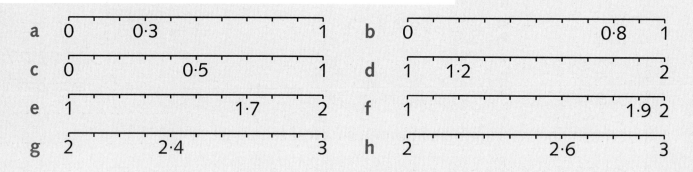

a 0   0·3   1   **b** 0   0·8   1

c 0   0·5   1   **d** 1   1·2   2

e 1   1·7   2   **f** 1   1·9   2

g 2   2·4   3   **h** 2   2·6   3

2 Draw a number line from 5 to 6. Fill in all the tenths.

　　a Which tenths round down to 5?　　**b** Which tenths round up to 6?

Challenge 2

1 Write the two whole numbers that each decimal comes between.

　　a 2·6　　　**b** 1·3　　　**c** 3·7　　　**d** 5·9　　　**e** 6·5

　　f 9·4　　　**g** 7·2　　　**h** 4·8　　　**i** 9·1　　　**j** 10·7

2 For each decimal number in Question 1, look at the tenths digit and decide whether the number should be rounded up or down. Circle the whole number the decimal rounds to.

Challenge 3

1 Write all nine decimal tenths that would be rounded down or up to each of these numbers.

　　a 2　　　**b** 5　　　**c** 7　　　**d** 3　　　**e** 6

　　f 10　　　**g** 13　　　**h** 15　　　**i** 16　　　**j** 24

2 Explain the rules for rounding tenths.

Sports day

Solve simple problems involving decimals to 1 place

Five children enter the long jump, the cross-country run and the 50 m sprint.

Long jump	
Name	Distance jumped
Helena	1·2 m
Robin	1·8 m
Maya	1·1 m
Fatima	0·9 m
Jake	1·5 m

Challenge 1

a Who jumped the furthest? How do you know?

b Put all the children in order of how far they jumped.

c Round all the children's distances to the nearest metre.

d Change all the distances to metres and fractions.

e Draw a number line like this and put all the children's distances on it.

0   1   2

Challenge 2

a Put all the runners in order of how far they ran.

b Round all the runners' distances to the nearest km.

c Maya said to Helena, "I only ran 0·1 km further than you, but when we round our distance it seems I ran 1 km further than you." Is this fair?

d Change all the distances to kilometres and fractions.

Cross-country run	
Name	Distance run
Helena	3·4 km
Robin	2·9 km
Maya	3·5 km
Fatima	3·1 km
Jake	2·7 km

Challenge 3

a Put all the runners in order of their time.

b Round all the runners' times to the nearest second.

c Helena said to Maya, "When our times are rounded to the nearest second, your time improves and mine does not." Why is this? Is it fair?

50 m sprint	
Name	Time
Helena	12·4 seconds
Robin	14·5 seconds
Maya	12·6 seconds
Fatima	13·3 seconds
Jake	14·8 seconds

Unit 3, Week 3, Lesson I

Recording mass using decimal notation

Record metric units for mass using decimals

Challenge 1

Write each mass in kilograms and grams.

a 2500 g   b 3100 g   c 5700 g   d 2900 g

Example

4600 g = 4 kg 600 g

Challenge 2

1 Write the mass of each chicken in four different ways.

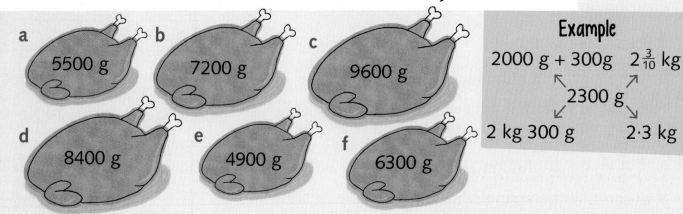

a 5500 g   b 7200 g   c 9600 g

d 8400 g   e 4900 g   f 6300 g

Example

2000 g + 300g $2\frac{3}{10}$ kg

2300 g

2 kg 300 g   2·3 kg

2 Write each mass in grams.

a 6·4 kg   b 8·5 kg   c 5·7 kg

d 13·1 kg   e 22·9 kg   f 17·6 kg

Example

7·2 kg = 7000 g + 200 g
        = 7200 g

3 Write the weights shown on these scales.

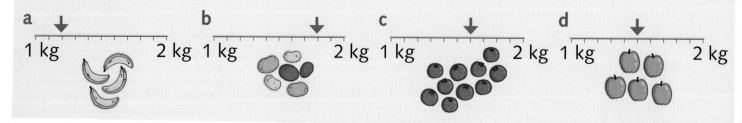

a   b   c   d
1 kg   2 kg 1 kg   2 kg 1 kg   2 kg 1 kg   2 kg

Challenge 3

Look at the scales in Challenge 2, Question 3. Find the approximate mass in grams of:

a 1 banana   b 1 potato   c 1 tomato   d 1 apple

36

Multiples of standard weights

Use multiplication to convert from larger to smaller units

Challenge 1

You have four standard weights.

Example

450 g = 2 × 200 g + 50 g

Write the least number of weights you need to balance the mass of each kitten. You can use each weight more than once.

a   350 g   b   140 g   c   470 g   d   290 g

Challenge 2

You have six standard weights. You can use each weight more than once to answer these questions.

Example

1 kg = 2 × 500 g

1   Balance 1 kg using: a   4 weights   b   5 weights   c   10 weights

2   Balance 500 g using: a   3 weights   b   5 weights   c   10 weights

3   Balance 100 g using: a   2 weights   b   4 weights   c   5 weights

4   Find four ways to balance 450 g using 50 g, 100 g and 200 g weights.

Challenge 3

1   How many different ways can you balance 750 g using 50 g, 100 g, 200 g and 500 g weights?

2   A baker has one 100 g weight and one 200 g weight. How can he use these weights to measure out 900 g of flour?

Estimating and rounding masses

Estimate and compare mass, and round numbers on scales

Challenge 1

Round the mass shown on each scale to the nearest kilogram.

   **a**      **b**      **c**      **d**

Example

8 kg

Challenge 2

1 Estimate the mass shown on each scale to the nearest 100 g.

   **a**   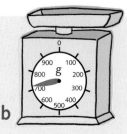   **b**   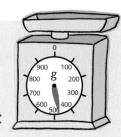   **c**   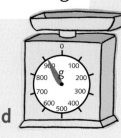   **d**

Example

just over
600 g

2 Round the mass shown on each scale to the nearest kilogram.

   **a**      **b**      **c**      **d**

Challenge 3

1 Copy and complete the table.

Mass in g	5700 g	3400 g	6800 g	3200 g	7500 g	4600 g
Mass in kg	5·7 kg					
Rounded to nearest kg	6 kg					

a Arrange the digits 3, 5 and 7 to make six different kilogram masses similar to the example.

b Round each mass to the nearest kilogram.

c Find the difference between the lightest and heaviest masses. Round your answer to the nearest kilogram.

Example

3   5 · 7 kg

Garden centre calculations

Calculate different measures of mass using decimals to 1 place

Terracotta pots are on special offer at the garden centre. A hyacinth bulb weighs 0·3 kg. Find the total mass in kilograms of:

0·8 kg   1·2 kg   1·6 kg

a 1 small pot and 1 bulb   **b** 1 medium pot and 3 bulbs   **c** 1 large pot and 5 bulbs

Each tray has 10 potted plants.

a 9·3 kg begonias   b 10·5 kg cyclamen   c 7·8 kg pansies   d 11·7 kg petunias

1 Round the mass of each tray of plants to the nearest whole kilogram.

2 For each tray, find the mass in grams of 1 potted plant.

3 Find the total mass of 1 tray of begonias and 1 tray of petunias.

4 How much heavier is a tray of cyclamen plants than a tray of pansies?

5 A keen gardener bought 30 pansies and 30 petunias.
   What was the total mass of his plants?

- A bag of compost and a bag of sand together weigh 25 kg.

- A bag of compost and a bag of grit together weigh 22·5 kg.

- A bag of sand and a bag of grit together weigh 17·5 kg.

Find the mass in kilograms of:

a a bag of compost   b a bag of sand   c a bag of grit

Square numbers

Recall square numbers to 12 x 12 and the related division facts

Challenge 1

Draw each of the square numbers in your book or on squared paper. Write the multiplication fact and related division fact for each.

Example

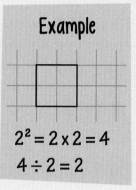

$2^2 = 2 \times 2 = 4$

$4 \div 2 = 2$

a 2^2 b 3^2 c 4^2 d 5^2

e 6^2 f 7^2 g 8^2 h 9^2

Challenge 2

Some of the square numbers are missing in this grid. Find the missing square numbers and write the multiplication and related division fact, starting with the smallest square number. The largest square number has been done for you.

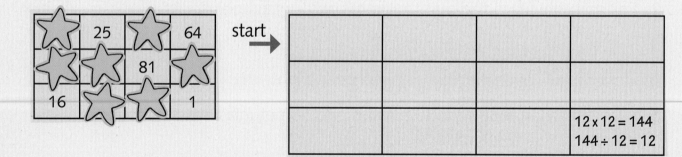

start →

			$12 \times 12 = 144$ $144 \div 12 = 12$

Grid (with stars): 25, 64 / 81 / 16, 1

Challenge 3

Work out the answers to these calculations about square numbers. Show your working.

Example

$6^2 + 5^2 =$ | 61

a $12^2 - 6^2 =$ _____   b $9^2 + 7^2 =$ _____   c $11^2 - 4^2 =$ _____

d $6^2 \times 2^2 =$ _____   e $8^2 \times 3^2 =$ _____   f $12^2 + 8^2 =$ _____

g $9^2 - 5^2 =$ _____   h $7^2 - 2^2 =$ _____   i $10^2 + 9^2 =$ _____

7 multiplication table

Recall the multiplication and division facts for the 7 multiplication table

1 Write the multiple of 7 that comes before each of these numbers.

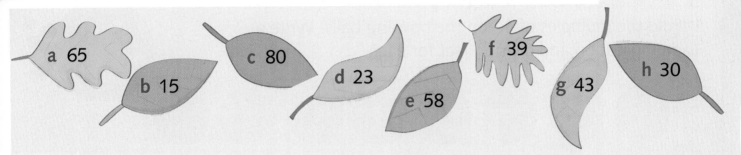

a 65

b 15

c 80

d 23

e 58

f 39

g 43

h 30

2 Write the multiples of 7 from 7 to 84 in order, smallest to largest.

Find the missing number in each calculation.

a $\square \times 7 = 49$

b $7 \times 0 = \triangle$

c $7 \times \triangle = 63$

d $\triangle \times 7 = 35$

e $12 \times \bullet = 84$

f $7 = 7 \times \square$

g $\blacksquare \times 7 = 21$

h $28 \div \square = 7$

i $56 \div \bigcirc = 8$

j $\bigcirc \div 1 = 7$

k $42 = \triangle \times 7$

l $14 \div \blacksquare = 2$

m $\square \div 7 = 11$

n $\square \times 7 = 70$

o $49 \div \triangle = 7$

Read the clues to find each number.

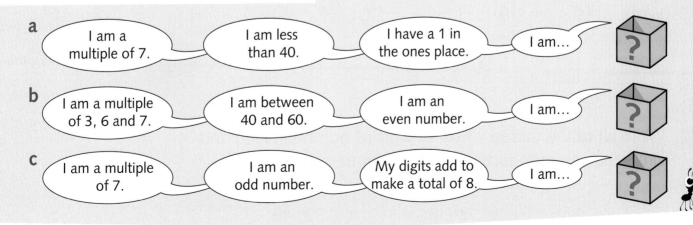

a I am a multiple of 7.   I am less than 40.   I have a 1 in the ones place.   I am…

b I am a multiple of 3, 6 and 7.   I am between 40 and 60.   I am an even number.   I am…

c I am a multiple of 7.   I am an odd number.   My digits add to make a total of 8.   I am…

Unit 4, Week 1, Lesson 3

Finding factors

- Recall the multiplication and division facts for the 11 and 12 multiplication tables
- Recognise and find factors of numbers to multiples up to 12 x 12

Challenge 1

1 Find the multiples of 11 on the bowling balls. Write a multiplication and division fact for each.

61 66 82 88 35 99 22 121

2 Find the multiples of 12. Write a multiplication and division fact for each.

36 60 64 144 92 132 72 86

Challenge 2

Find the factors of the number on each bowling ball from the numbers given on the skittles.

a 20 — 2 3 7 4 6 10
b 28 — 3 4 6 7 8 12
c 18 — 5 3 4 6 9 8
d 35 — 3 5 6 8 7 11
e 30 — 2 4 6 5 3 9
f 60 — 3 7 5 10 12 9

Challenge 3

Write all of the factors of these pairs of numbers. Find and circle the common factors of both numbers.

a 24, 16   b 36, 64   c 32, 48

42

Solving problems using multiples

Solve problems involving multiplication and division facts

allenge 1

These multiples are all jumbled up. Sort them into multiples of 3, 8, 9 and 12.

6 18 27 24 30   16 56 32   54 36 72   144 108 60

allenge 2

Use the doubling strategy shown to write the answer to each 12 multiplication calculation.

a   4 × 12   b   10 × 12   c   3 × 12

d   7 × 12   e   6 × 12   f   9 × 12

g   12 × 12   h   8 × 12   i   11 × 12

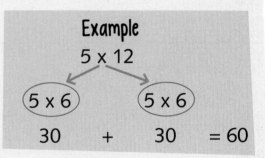

Example

5 × 12

5 × 6   5 × 6

30   +   30   = 60

allenge 3

Sort the multiples into the correct section in each Venn diagram.

a   24, 27, 36, 40, 32, 21, 15, 11

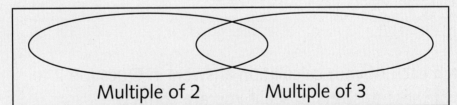

Multiple of 2   Multiple of 3

b   16, 20, 32, 40, 25, 35, 44, 28

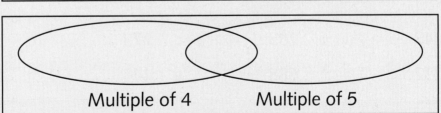

Multiple of 4   Multiple of 5

c   12, 18, 22, 36, 56, 48, 24, 15

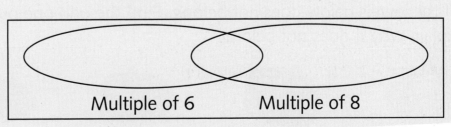

Multiple of 6   Multiple of 8

Multiplication using partitioning

Use partitioning to calculate multiplication of TO × O

Challenge 1

Write the multiples of 10 that come before and after these numbers.

| a | 73 | b | 37 | c | 87 | d | 26 | e | 62 |
| f | 11 | g | 48 | h | 49 | i | 55 | j | 94 |

Challenge 2

1 Write an approximate answer for each of these calculations.

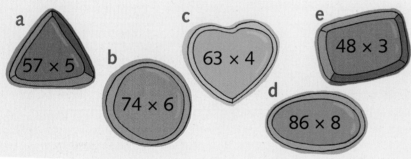

a 57 × 5
b 74 × 6
c 63 × 4
d 86 × 8
e 48 × 3
f 39 × 7
g 27 × 9
h 87 × 6

2 For each of the calculations in Question 1,
use partitioning to work out the answer.
Then check your answer with your estimate.

Example

63 × 8 = (60 × 8) + (3 × 8)
      =   480   +   24
      =   504

3 Match each of your calculation answers in Question 2 to
one of these answers to see if you are correct.

| a | 243 | b | 285 | c | 273 | d | 522 |
| e | 252 | f | 688 | g | 444 | h | 144 |

Challenge 3

One of the jewels below does not belong. Find the odd one out
and explain why it does not belong.

a  64 × 6
b  48 × 8
c 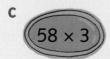 58 × 3
d  96 × 4

Multiplication using partitioning and the grid method

Use partitioning and the grid method to calculate multiplication of TO × O

llenge 1

Partition these numbers into 10s and 1s.

Example

$42 = 40 + 2$

a
57
43
16
39

Tens | Ones

b
83
68
26
91

Tens | Ones

c
59
47
64
76

Tens | Ones

llenge 2

1 Write an approximate answer for each of these calculations.

a 37×4 b 56×9 c 68×3 d 46×8 e 58×7 f 84×6

2 For each of these calculations, use the grid method to work out the answer.

Example

63×8

×	60	3	
8	480	24	= 504

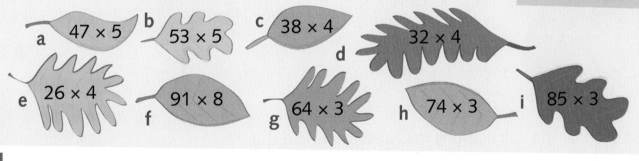

a 47×5
b 53×5
c 38×4
d 32×4
e 26×4
f 91×8
g 64×3
h 74×3
i 85×3

allenge 3

Some children used number cards and a 0–9 dice to make some calculations. They worked out the answers. Rahul forgot to write the number from the dice in each of his calculations. Can you work out which number he rolled?

a $43 \times \square = 215$ b $38 \times \bigcirc = 342$ c $76 \times \triangle = 532$

d $57 \times \triangle = 228$ e $89 \times \blacksquare = 534$ f $68 \times \bigcirc = 544$

Multiplication using the expanded written method

Use the expanded written method to calculate multiplication of TO × O

Challenge 1

Partition these numbers into 10s and 1s.

Example

87 = 80 + 7

a 45	b 38	c 63	d 56
e 74	f 82	g 27	h 94

Challenge 2

1 Write an approximate answer for each of these calculations.

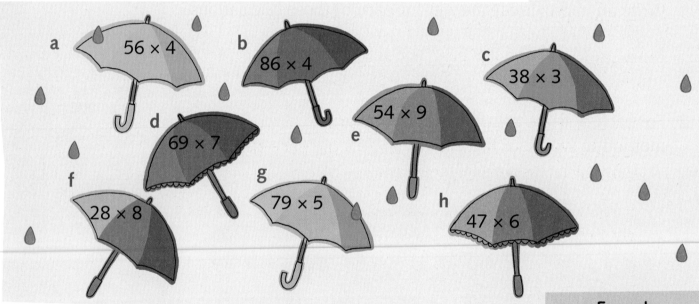

a 56 × 4

b 86 × 4

c 38 × 3

d 69 × 7

e 54 × 9

f 28 × 8

g 79 × 5

h 47 × 6

2 For each of the calculations in Question 1, use the expanded written method to work out the answer. Then check your answer with your estimate.

Example

```
  H T O
    6 3
×     8
─────────
    2 4    (3 × 8)
  4 8 0    (60 × 8)
─────────
  5 0 4
  1
```

Challenge 3

Choose three of your calculations from Challenge 2. Write a word problem to match.

Mental multiplications

- Recall multiplication facts
- Multiply together three numbers

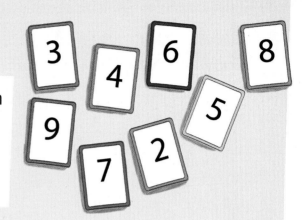

Challenge 1

- Choose two number cards. Write a multiplication calculation and work out the answer.

- Repeat this for four more calculations. You must use each card at least once.

Challenge 2

a $3 \times 5 \times 8$	b $2 \times 8 \times 4$	c $6 \times 5 \times 7$	d $8 \times 9 \times 10$
e $7 \times 7 \times 0$	f $9 \times 6 \times 3$	g $6 \times 4 \times 9$	h $9 \times 7 \times 1$
i $9 \times 5 \times 3$	j $2 \times 9 \times 5$	k $6 \times 10 \times 7$	l $4 \times 6 \times 4$

Challenge 3

1
- Choose three number cards. Write a multiplication calculation and work out the answer.

- Repeat this for four more calculations. You must use each card at least once.

2 Which three consecutive 1-digit numbers multiply together to make these answers?

    a 120   b 24   c 504   d 60

47

Converting units of time

Convert between different units of time

Challenge 1

Copy and complete using numbers from the circles.

1 min = ☐ s

1 hour = ☐ min

1 day = ☐ h

1 week = ☐ days

1 year = ☐ months

1 year = ☐ weeks

1 year = ☐ days

(24) (60) (365) (7) (12) (60) (52)

Challenge 2

1 Write how many minutes there are in:

   a 4 h   **b** 6 h   **c** $8\frac{3}{4}$ h

Example

5 h = 5 x 60 min
    = 300 min

2 Write how many hours there are in:

   a 5 days   **b** 9 days   **c** 15 days

3 Write how many days there are in:

   a 7 weeks   **b** 12 weeks   **c** 52 weeks

4 Convert these times.

   a 50 h to days and hours   **b** 200 m to hours and minutes

   c 400 s to minutes and seconds   **d** 60 days to weeks and days

Challenge 3

1 For the months of April, May and June, find the combined number of:

   a days   **b** weeks

2 Write the age you are today in years, months and days.

Written methods – addition

Example: 2456 + 5378

```
    2 4 5 6
 +  5 3 7 8
 ─────────
    7 8 3 4
        1 1
```

Written methods – subtraction

Example: 6418 – 2546

```
   5 13 11
   6̷ 4̷ 1̷ 8
 – 2  5  4  6
 ──────────
   3  8  7  2
```

Number facts

x	2	3	4	5	6	7	8	9	10	11	12
1	2	3	4	5	6	7	8	9	10	11	12
2	4	6	8	10	12	14	16	18	20	22	24
3	6	9	12	15	18	21	24	27	30	33	36
4	8	12	16	20	24	28	32	36	40	44	48
5	10	15	20	25	30	35	40	45	50	55	60
6	12	18	24	30	36	42	48	54	60	66	72
7	14	21	28	35	42	49	56	63	70	77	84
8	16	24	32	40	48	56	64	72	80	88	96
9	18	27	36	45	54	63	72	81	90	99	108
10	20	30	40	50	60	70	80	90	100	110	120
11	22	33	44	55	66	77	88	99	110	121	132
12	24	36	48	60	72	84	96	108	120	132	144

Written methods – multiplication

Example: 356 x 7

Partitioning

356 x 7 = (300 x 7) + (50 x 7) + (6 x 7)
= 2100 + 350 + 42
= 2492

Grid method

x	300	50	6	
7	2100	350	42	= 2492

Expanded written method

```
    3 5 6
 ×      7
 ─────────
     4 2  (  6 x 7)
   3 5 0  ( 50 x 7)
 2 1 0 0  (300 x 7)
 ─────────
 2 4 9 2
```

Formal written method

```
    3 5 6
 ×  ₃₄ 7
 ─────────
 2 4 9 2
```

Written methods – division

Example: 486 ÷ 9

Partitioning

486 ÷ 9 = (450 ÷ 9) + (36 ÷ 9)
= 50 + 4
= 54

Formal written method

```
    5 4
 9)4 8 ³6
```

Expanded written method

```
      5 4
 9) 4 8 6
    4 5 0   50 × 9
    ─────
      3 6
      3 6   4 × 9
    ─────
        0
```

Fractions and decimals

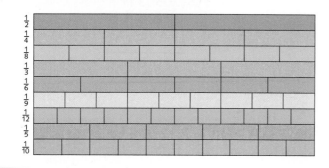

$$\frac{1}{100} = 0{\cdot}01$$

$$\frac{2}{100} = \frac{1}{50} = 0{\cdot}02$$

$$\frac{5}{100} = \frac{1}{20} = 0{\cdot}05$$

$$\frac{10}{100} = \frac{1}{10} = 0{\cdot}1$$

$$\frac{20}{100} = \frac{1}{5} = 0{\cdot}2$$

$$\frac{25}{100} = \frac{1}{4} = 0{\cdot}25$$

$$\frac{50}{100} = \frac{1}{2} = 0{\cdot}5$$

$$\frac{75}{100} = \frac{3}{4} = 0{\cdot}75$$

$$\frac{100}{100} = 1$$

Measurement

Length
1 kilometre (km) = 1000 metres (m)

0·1 km = 100 m

1 m = 100 centimetres (cm) = 1000 millimetres (mm)

0·1 m = 10 cm = 100 mm

1 cm = 10 mm

0·1 cm = 1 mm

Mass
1 kilogram (kg) = 1000 grams (g)

0·1 kg = 100g

0·01 kg = 10 g

Time
1 year = 12 months

= 356 days

= 366 days (leap year)

1 week = 7 days

1 day = 24 hours

1 hour = 60 minutes

1 minute = 60 seconds

Capacity
1 litre (*l*) = 1000 millilitres (ml)

0·1 *l* = 100 ml

0·01 *l* = 10 ml

30 days has September, April, June and November. All the rest have 31, except February alone which has 28 days clear and 29 in each leap year.

12-hour clock

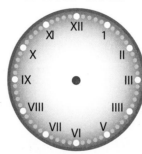

24-hour clock

Properties of shape

2-D shapes

 circle

 semi-circle

 right-angled triangle

 equilateral triangle

 isosceles triangle

 scalene triangle

 square

 rectangle

 Rhombus

 Kite

Parallelogram

 Trapezium

 pentagon

 hexagon

 heptagon

 octagon

3-D shapes

 cube

 cuboid

 cone

 cylinder

 sphere

 hemi-sphere

 triangular prism

 triangular-based pyramid (tetrahedron)

 square-based pyramid

Angles

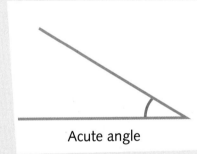
Acute angle

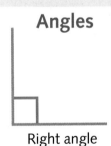
Right angle

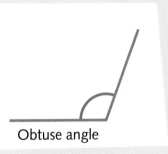
Obtuse angle

Position and direction

Coordinates

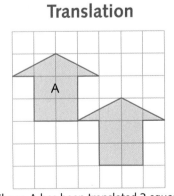

Translation

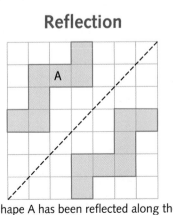

Shape A has been translated 3 squares to the right and 2 squares down.

Reflection

Shape A has been reflected along the diagonal line of symmetry.